UNIVERSAL CORNER

ALSO BY MITCHELL L. H. DOUGLAS

dying in the scarecrow's arms
\blak\\al-fə bet
Cooling Board: A Long-Playing Poem

Universal Corner

POEMS

Mitchell L. H. Douglas

A Karen & Michael Braziller Book
PERSEA BOOKS / NEW YORK

Persea Books, Inc.
90 Broad Street
New York, New York 10004

LIBRARY OF CONGRESS CATALOGING-IN-PUBLICATION DATA

Names: Douglas, Mitchell L. H., 1970– author
    Title: Universal corner : poems / Mitchell L. H. Douglas.
Description: New York : Persea Books, 2026. | Summary: "Dancing at the intersection of melody and humanity, Mitchell L. H. Douglas' Universal Corner imagines what beat moves the world. Douglas' poetry rides the skip and pop of vinyl, radio waves, and mixtape collage through a complex modern life, his voice equally shaped by freestyling and stage diving, having come of age in two seemingly different musical cultures: punk and Hip-Hop. These seemingly disparate genres reveal surprising connections in Douglas' poems, in which he finds that, through the experience of memory and musical communion, common ground abounds. Reconciling rage and joy, public and private, Mitchell Douglas is one of our most vital voices of the urban Midwest, a poet of with both a critical and compassionate perspective on the pulse of America's heartland"—Provided by publisher.
Identifiers: LCCN 2025044836 (print) | LCCN 2025044837 (ebook) |
    ISBN 9780892556335 paperback | ISBN 9780892556342 ebk
Subjects: LCGFT: Poetry
Classification: LCC PS3604.O9323 U55 2026 (print) | LCC PS3604.O9323 (ebook)
    | DDC 811/.6—dc23/eng/20251121
LC record available at https://lccn.loc.gov/2025044836
LC ebook record available at https://lccn.loc.gov/2025044837

Book design and composition by Rita Skingle
Typeset in Adobe Jenson Pro
Manufactured in the United States of America.
Printed on acid-free paper.

For Dad,
Save me a cloud close to you.

"Daniel, you're a star in the face of the sky"
—ELTON JOHN

"You may be flying through the air
wrapped up in how high you can go"
—LABELLE

"Like Icarus ascending on beautiful foolish arms . . ."
—JONI MITCHELL

Radio Free Iowa

"Always wear shoes that are good for running or fighting."
　　　—JOE STRUMMER

　　　　　　　　Let the dirt turn the dial, the dew-slick
sheen of grass land the tune that tells. This is the story of my body,

its new-teen year. No time to climb,
　　　　　　　　　　　　tonight we leap: free

of the box, its plastic mysticisms, feedback & growl—often in the form
of shout, often like the voices gnaw now. Free of the radio, my hands

reach for fences, the spell of open spaces,　　　　　propel
my Black　　　　　　　　　　　to flight.

I.

"The new sounds are there if somebody wants to listen."

—ERIC DOLPHY, liner notes, *Outward Bound*

Our Youth, Oh Lord, Burns Longer Than the Night

. . . it's like that time we saw N.W.A. @ Louisville Gardens because we would buy anything that rhymed no matter what coast it claimed, & this dude nobody knew took the stage by his damn self & rocked it: Kings hat cocked, a leather trench, & jeans sagging past his boxers through every Dre/laced/drum. & N.W.A. bum rushed the stage like a Public Enemy hook, all black & motion, an all-Black commotion, & after "Straight Outta Compton" laid the stage to waste, we found ourselves outside stumbling through the luminescent dark, our voices aimed as coos toward a tour bus where J.J. Fad stood in the stairwell laughing off our come-ons through closed doors. Until the see-through walls parted & the Brother No One Knew Who Rocked the Stage By His Damn Self knifed the night sky w/ his Kings cap, put his hand on my shoulder, & launched himself into the corner light, away from where we were never invited in. & if we had been, what? What did 15-year-old us know what to say to three rhyming queens from a land we'd never seen? Younger than young, bluegrass breath— & still, the hours blaze.

Folk Art

(for Bill Withers)

His voice is the radio. Momma
drifts the Sherman Minton, exits

New Albany to child's play
in Kentucky. We rise & defy. Four

seats & us two
ramble across the river.

This far o'er the Ohio, the only current
is sound, the churn of guitar

& a deacon's tone bless
our ears, the white Opel: jewel

of a ride from another time. Another day
means one more chance for anything.

Dawn ropes my conscience,
Bill's voice: sweet charm

of gold. We cradle him
in the squawk of car speakers, tales

about the hands of a matriarch
like the one a river away.

All through the day arithmetic
puzzles me, comic books a breeze,

& spelling tests, spelling tests . . .
be gone already.

I can be a mess of a boy, forget
it's picture day & show up in my uniform,

or think it's field day & come to school
in street clothes. "Street" clothes

makes me laugh, like the fabric
is as rough as the roads we ride.

Fierce about my time, give me
a ball & a court, no nets required. Give me

a bike to sneak
off the block, a synthezoid

of green & gold, his blue fur friend. Tell me
one day math will make sense,

that addition & subtraction can feel as good
as phasing through walls, me

minus restriction, the world one sound & shape.
Let the radio play.

Declaration

We declare our deaths
redundant, the surrender

of flesh & breath an absence
already of this earth. There are other worlds

we've seen, times we've tilled
& harvested, long green sights

that stoke a hunger: deep
twisted root of a thing, the vines

that refuse to wither, the winter
of denial. You keep telling me

Die,   & I laugh
in your face, your arsenic

gasp, rasp
w/in an inch,

w/out mask,
& I believe

you can't trust science
when all signs say

One Way. I refuse
the casket & the day-

dream, the home-
going like ash-

long menthol, burning me up
from the inside. I have learned

what to share & what to keep—never
parse my heart,

offer no morsel
to cannibals.

Excursions

The child bouncing a basketball up the sidewalk
past your bedroom window does not know
your first class starts @ noon, how many minutes you pray
to keep your eyes tight

before your phone turns
to bell. No.
They've got a park to see, a corner
to turn, & this flat thud

abusing the pavement is your new
alarm. You're welcome,
lazy. Get up
& greet the morning. Don't

let children have all the fun.
You've forgotten what it means
to be young. How far away
you've wondered. Your imagination

stunted by faculty meetings
& annual reports. You light candles
for summer break, let incense clouds billow
beneath your office door—hope no one

narcs you out to the Chair. In class, you lecture

that lines should never break
after articles. Save that
for sensory nouns & active verbs
you say. Heads bob on the surface
of silence. For the final project,

an assignment to create a new form, a student
raises his hand. Says all
40 lines of his poem
will break

on a,
an,
& the.

Poem that Begins w/a Tweet
About Gwendolyn Brooks

Gwendolyn Brooks was a Jeopardy question no one could answer tonight.
That's a metaphor too painful to wrap my head around.

& I said, *The poem is about Love*
because all poems are about Love,

& you rolled your eyes so hard
I thought they would snap back to center

w/cherries & diamonds. The flit
of your lashes renders me nameless & I fall

blank for what feels like a block. Falling
is a metaphor for my life: unsettled,

unmoored. I capitalize Love
because it is bigger than what we are

or what we give credit for: oaken,
open. For that, you have no answer,

your breath in kitchenettes:
hal/ved, qu/art/er/ed—cut again.

It's a Demo

You don't know this, but Steady B was the only one
who took the time. Terminator X looked @ me

like his fist should be connected to my jaw
when I slipped him a TDK & told him the name

of my crew was R²PE (Radically Raged
Posse in Effect). The '80s were cruel

to slang & fashion, so was Reagan,
but he's not allowed here. Steady B, on tour

w/MC Lyte, took the chalice of plastic,
sat down on his bed—his ear

to a boom box—while Tat Money talked to girls
who wouldn't look @ us twice.   Two times the fire

years later in the North of Death, a PNC,
the officer (mother) vs. Cool C on the trigger—

not as cool as we thought. B @ the wheel
going nowhere. Who cares if we weren't stars?

Hardheaded Man

@ Christmas, I tell my wife
who will soon be my ex,

Every time I see
Granddaddy, it's like

he's trying to tell me
everything he knows.

By summer,
he can't speak.

       I want the sound back.

Never thought the voice
would leave

before the vessel. I want to say
he knew,

that even if he couldn't name
his fate, he felt his body

shift, fall
like a soft riverbank, each day

a climb back to the surface.
It comes back to me:

Granddaddy wheelchair-bound,
his mouth open, lung

½ collapsed, his absent words
a form betraying content. Pictures of him

in red suspenders, Grandmamma
by his side, their Selma fairytale

behind glass. The day I stay
to feed him food that isn't

hers: mashed turkey & green beans,
remnants of the last meal

hidden in his mouth. He tries
to work the bits of meat

off curve of lip
to spit, still

no words. Restless, arms
rise & hug the air,

someone lost or in wait,
someone we are not

meant to see. I try
not to look

@ the smiling picture,
snap the capture.

That feels like a hand
in his mouth,

a muzzled tongue.
                    Don't laugh

when I say I've seen this in others,
that I come from a people w/more eyes

than options. No parlor trick:
a chest balloons, the labor

of breath, & a feeling beyond your body
that someone you love

lowered the oars.

Seer

(for Devonte Hart)

You can't have this body; there is no blue
that can soak my weight, sink
my heart. I want to be free. See me flying

on a distant wave, hat blown to the wind
in the sheer force of now. I don't want to be
somebody, I am somebody—I'm just waiting

for you to notice. There was a time
when I smiled, the curl of my lips a bow
pulled tight for flight. Things are different now:

there are two faces, two mothers, a whole
lot of empty. I wasn't crying for the reason
you think I was crying, & why couldn't anyone

who ever loved a child see? If you never find me
brown & buoyant against the current, know that I move
like the dreams of boys held under water. In other words,

I move like the dreams of boys held under. I move
like the dreams of boys held. I move like the dreams
of boys. I move like the dreams. I move like

American Top 40

You're not sure why, but every week some new band chats it up w/Dick Clark on Saturday TV & you hear them the next day on KRNA, Casey Kasem's cartoon voice introducing the latest song you're supposed to care about. Even that short guy w/the perm who answers questions w/fingers to Clark's face & no sound, a silent movie. In fact, he holds four in the air, flare to a query forgotten. One new moon, it will be the punchline when someone asks how many times you saw him play before the pills took him & his mention on the dial birthed memorial instead of dance floor. Radio doesn't top your list of priorities; you're 11. You want to play baseball—professionally, not w/these little league losers. You want birthday parties where even the kids you don't like give presents you may or may not use. The year kids come w/footballs (the gift guessed before unwrapping) your best friend offers *Never Mind the Bollocks*, pink & green cover safety pinning your psyche. You crave noise—to be live, front & center, lost by choice in another signal—head shaved, sharp as your new bright mind.

Artifacts

Somehow, Aaliyah loses
her graded quiz in your yard, a B–, perhaps
the sting of which she wasn't keen
on carting home. Printed on green, still
not camouflaged in the lawn, standing out
like a sore grade. Better

than what you usually find: plastic
airplane bottles minus
the alcohol, what used to be

a pack of menthols, Styrofoam
containers w/out the food, a refuge
for missing parts. Still,

a B– seems out of place,
like an encore
no one asked for. Do you live in a magnet

for the abandoned?   Does the child
want more from the mark? The teacher–
pen bleeding–ignores the brilliance

in the penciled architecture
of their pupil's name: exalted.
You make copies

of the castaway w/more green paper, fold
& stack around the perimeter. Your neighbors say,
"B–, that's not so bad." The litter stops, the grass

grows, & dogs sniff
your new paper fence, bark
for what is no longer allowed,

the feel of it—rest, release.
A borrowed space, your curious
museum.

In Utero

Don't you remember
when ODB broke into "Shimmy Shimmy Ya,"
the crowd lurched left, broke a foot
off in the dance floor, & your mother
cradled the thought of you in one hand,
the other a fist
raised to midnight? You
served a late-night kick, caught
in bass knock, the thump
of an MC's voice,
"Yeah baby, I like it rawwwwww . . ."

) Oh, you're thinking
that one. If there was Fender
feedback, wild solo
& swing of a Mustang
set to stun,
it would go here—some finesse
behind the boards à la Albini, even.
Why not—dream (

. . . the piano loop jangles.

      Don't you remember the sister, black
dress wrapped, mixing screwdrivers on stage
while Big Baby Jesus got higher? Don't you
remember the heat a crowd holds,
the euphoric combustion?

Isn't it still in your walk?
"Brooklyn Zoo"
every twist
of your locs?

To the Man Who Flipped Me the Bird
from a Bicycle Not Once But Twice in the
Middle of Ditch Road While I Sat in My Car

Know how it works. Title the poem "To the Man Who Flipped Me the Bird from a Bicycle Not Once but Twice in the Middle of Ditch Road While I Sat in My Car" & let the reader run ragged. There is a metaphor for you to glean, something to comb through like karma. There's got to be subtext here. I am not a formula, there is more than one right answer (which of course is there is no right answer & no one to save you from this poem). I'm so mad I could spit. What do you want? Gave me the finger is such a funny phrase—no foul or high wire act, certainly nothing that tips it hat @ skill. Remember Ferlinghetti, the balance in the lines, teetering against the question of reason? I wonder . . . was it the unsolicited addendum of digits . . . of gifts . . . excuse me—are you writing this down? He—back straight on a bike in the middle of Ditch—a street that sounds like a trap— leveled his hand like a weapon, steadied it in my line of sight, then did it again just to make sure I knew what I was dealing w/, that I had, in fact, been told to fuck off (another phrase to laugh @). Thank God I was parked, just stared instead of leaving the lane for a hydrant, dying of questions instead of splitting trees. But you & I both know the horror of trees, don't we? Especially in Indiana. Dare you add another tale to the bark, become the sacred severed—trophy in skin.

Persimmons

Our state, our comfort—a sweet strange.
Offered in a pudding by my professor on our first meeting, a café on
Kirkwood before the start of the semester. "Try it," he says, "it's a local favorite." I am
not a local, though I've known poems in states w/ I's & enough white skin to make
my breath anomaly, so I get the gist quick: campus is oasis, step outside & it's Outer
Limits. I make friends, the only male poet admitted my year. Funny to say now (what
stumbling pride for gender). Others follow, including KY ties. I am shocked to hear a
friend admitted the year after me is shut down in workshop over a poem about lynching.
"Hasn't everything about lynching already been said?" fired a mouth
I thought knew better. Have we stopped dying? It's a matter of the pulp & the rendering,
how to reap what lies beneath the papery skin, forget the seeds.
Years later, the friend says, "Mitch, you are a roach; you could
live anywhere." Plant, uproot, repeat.
I suppose there is truth to this, true that I adapt—survive.
How I keep my curiosity on the way to heartwood, think of her beaten poem,
& look up the last IN lynching   on the books: 1930,   Marion, not so long ago
that the memory
is smoke. The photographs that survive of the men who didn't,
the proud Hoosier as vector pointing skyward,

finger & smirk

an arrow over

shoulder.

As if to say,

"Would you look @ that—   three plump bulbs   ripe in the twine."

II.

"Used to be an Experience meant making you
a bit older. This one makes you wider."

—THE JIMI HENDRIX EXPERIENCE,
liner notes, *Are You Experienced?*

Radio Free Iowa

              How
did we get here? A bottle
thrown over a fence, plastic

@ our feet. The bottle thrown back—
the street filled w/ Izod & Polo in reply,
staring us down like Socs

in an S. E. Hinton novel. No longer
fiction, outnumbered 5 to 1. Nothing to do
but run.

Darby Crash Calls a Dead Painter a W———k
& I Rethink My Adolescence

because I want to believe @ 13 I didn't know
what this spit & cinder was, that I scrawled
We Must Bleed across the back
of a Hawkeyes Rose Bowl T-shirt & shanked it
w/safety pins in 8th grade ignorance. Because
he was drunk & wanting more—a place
I've been—& he wailed
like a wounded manimal
from a low-slung stage, braved bottles
& spit & the imminent destruction
of his pale, pale body.

       How did I miss
the slur from our spike-haired protagonist, his majesty
of beer & leather, Penelope's zoom
& focus over the frying-pan slap of bacon & eggs,
Darby's companion recalling the incident w/glee:
the man thought to be asleep,
but not. The man dead—his house
painting incomplete; the pictures they took
crowding around the corpse of someone
loved, a ghost already angered
w/out a foot in the grave.

       How else
could I dance the halls of Southeast Jr. High,
a Strummer-wide mohawk battering
the path, the drawl of *Caught in my eye, yeah*
dragged through the pale air
like the unbroken song of aerosol? I want to believe
I made you a hero—poster child of saints
Angst & Oppression—out of the absence

of knowledge, that no book or ear turned me
in the name of freedom. Do not be mistaken:
I was not free. I was not the razor,
the independent thinker, hell—that mohawk
wasn't even my idea. I wore it
like I wore your lyrics: against my body (the opposite
of pale), against my questions, my parents'
wishes. Always against, open,
seen. Always a sword
no matter the livery.

                    * * *

When the trucker kept drinking
& got behind the wheel—numb
in the spirit— he slammed
his tractor trailer into the car
that never brought Bill's mother
home. The company threw money
@ his feet & Bill tried to make it, bought a farm
safe from the streets where jocks & rednecks
chased us, gave I.C. punks
some peace. & love thrived, our pack
a little braver, house parties & talk
of our own bands, Black Flag
& beer bottles rattling our ears.

"How about a mohawk?"

Bill said, my parents
out of town & my head
laid bare to the breath
of winter.

Joist

In the heat of the summer, the house grows
         a belly. We walk on its swell, fall back
into surfaces—pillows, arms. When you visit,
         you become its walls, what makes the space

a place I need. Let me be silent in the gut
         of this house, rise when it rises, open the door
if & only if I'm needed outside. My mother
         suggests that it's more than heat. "Maybe

the house has secrets," she says. What house
         doesn't? The problem here
is that this house has been doing so much
         talking lately. It can't keep

its mouth—its floor—shut.
         I'm used to silence. Keep hiding
from me. If I can't bear the pain,
         I don't want to know.

My Student Says, "Damn, Prof. Where Are All the Happy Poems?"

& I have to tell them the tale we all fear. There was a time when poets smiled, smoked
cigarettes @ readings, & nothing was ever touched after a first draft. Some called it
Nirvana, some Mecca. Then the drama

started. Who knew the word Mecca would unearth all those bigots (JK—we knew)?
It was a long war as wars often are. Both sides decimated in the desire to be right
when only one was. Editors trembled

(then ignored telegrams). We writhed in the pages of unwritten love poems. Book burning
became fashion. You bragged about attendance like Hoosiers @ lyn . . . it was a state
no one wanted, like New Jersey. Forgive me,

I couldn't resist. I've never been to the Garden State, but I love the poets there—
the poeming in their slightly/sorely blood-laced dirt.   This is a cry for help, a stab
wound & the stitches meant to heal. "Enough of the telling,"

my student says, "show me everything." *Listen*, I plead, *sometimes, a poem doesn't know
its own power. Sometimes, a line break*

is the state of a heart.

To My Daughter, 12, Who Says She Is Afraid of Police

Youngest: you are right
to trust your gut—it's never let you
down before. Your name

could mean girl who floats
instead of walks, girl who
says "I'm an artist" w/out

prompt—freedom, the living
question: girl
who dreams & sees the flame

come true. It could mean
all these things because all
these things are you,

but quite simply, it means purpose—
not because you are simple,
but because we wanted you

to have one. & all of this floods
my mind in the heat-drawn haze
of summer, wanting more for you

than fear, more than a scream
strapped to some stranger's power,
their house of cards

boxing your breath
on nights meant for a wish
& open window. Because

we still owe a debt
for your deliverance.
Because our eyes work

& everything is on camera.

"Slow farm tractor flees police, setting off slow speed chase"

Associated Press headline, June 21, 2018

First of all, there's no such thing
as fleeing police (they want,
they snuff), nor does the word "chase" exist
@ low speed. There is only
meandering a puzzled path

forward, stumbling a road
that cuts cornfields, buoyed
atop rubber monoliths crop circles
envy—some kind of country
god.   & the cops,

how hard did they laugh
@ the farmer turned gangster who said
"Fuck this,"
& floored it to 3;   3—
w/a combine strapped to the back

& his future hotter than July,
the sun's relentless peck
courting his neck,
& sirens whistling
through the wheat.

Mala

Maybe when we talk
@ the end of this divided date,
we won't mention the shooting
@ the synagogue in CA, six months

to the day after the shooting
@ the synagogue in PA.
We'll just chat about our children,
& movies, & our life

of love ahead. This one you've spent
threading prayer beads, this one
you've wrapped in the blessing
of emerald, cat's eye—heart

chakra—& shouldn't that
be enough? One dusk
when our voice never turns
to blood?

                Push it away—
@ least for the night. Won't death
                still be death
in the morning? Let the sun

bleat its hot brass
second line, let the black birds
be jealous. Let the grass—

      a blade,

      a bead,

a blade—

weep
for joy.

ATL

The set implodes when ODB does the most ODB thing ever: he falls headfirst
into a tirade no one can decipher. A Wu line nine-mics strong becomes a show

    w/in a show, stares quizzically @ itself, then falls apart like a fake
Cuban link. All this before Rage takes the stage, before de la Rocha

        commands all your revolutionary ire w/the spit
        of "Down Rodeo," a wave of heads nodding

        on one beat. You see MTV cameras came to catch it all,
you see your first wife & the friend who will be her second

        act fall back from the rock. Admit it: you are good
        @ missing the obvious, the drama that sets fires

        instead of blowing kisses. What did Dad used to say,
        the way he asked for something close enough to kill

            & you walked on by?
            If it was a snake . . .

Poetry & I Are Seeing Other People

Poetry has a partner, a side piece, & a million
excuses. Poetry wonders if you noticed
that it's gaining weight

in all the wrong phrases. Poetry
looked @ you w/a straight em dash
& said "Does my break look fat

in this stanza?" Poetry
has a new diet plan
that will make their partner jealous. Poetry

lost their side piece because they got tired
of Poetry's empty promises
& commitmentphobia. Poetry is, in fact, a freak

in the sheets & the streets. Poetry will get you
drunk, tell you about the time
it didn't want to write poetry no more, hope

you forget when you're sober. Poetry
is a dramatic little tart. Forgive them. Poetry
said fuck you if you not a believer—

you can catch these hands. Poetry
will catch you slipping & tell on you
before you can tell on yourself. Poetry is your ride

or die, your two-piece w/a biscuit, & your five
on it. Poetry got a crew called The Dirty Sonnets
a.k.a. the Baker's Dozen

because they're a little extra
& just that nice. Poetry said, Look,
there's one spot left.   It's yours

if you're down.
& you said, *Let me think about it*,
to which Poetry replied

"Shiiiiiiiiiiiiiiiiiiiiiiiiiiiiiiit,"
snatched the spot back,
your wig attached.

Ekphrasis: The Cover of Bad Brains'
Quickness as a Map to Light

Ever wandered the discomfort a stare unfolds, eyes piercing their way into unnamed tomorrows? Who holds that gaze? Only those w/power & here are four. All that gangsta plaid on D.C. Rastas: map of SE x NW, the pearl/plastic button trail on HR's shirt that reveals itself as the whispered opulence of God. A vision in B&W the year you graduate high school w/bands the world would talk about, & you share halls. It takes years before you start your own, before you finally meet HR face to face, mumble something about his influence as he drinks in your praise w/a nod & faux yardie Patois. Everything is frozen & cartoon—how? How do you trace, animate leap & SRO hush in one lush life? @ their core, they are fusion: the chops for jazz, a chemical reaction, the nucleus of hardened existence. Punker than punk, if that's possible. Hardcore is backflip, & sing-along, & honor badge bruise, & Black, & Black, &

Mic Control

(for David Jolicoeur)

Trugoy wasn't w/it: an unsanctioned inter-
view hours before the stage

& the mic he would rock. Me
too young to know

these kinds of arrangements
were typically, yes, arranged: the tape

empty, nothing
but false starts, his pacing, a long island

from inquiry. If this works,
then what? *Vibe? Spin? Rolling Stone?* The kid

that got on
by taking the risk, the new

demo tape: pen swing.
      The show went on, Plug

One, Plug Two . . . Dave in the distance,
got this interview

out of focus. Locked
in like the best MC:

off the dome, nothing
that paper can hold.

For Luck

Hoppin' John & kale because collards were nowhere to be found. Wedge of cornbread like a divided sun, no pork this year. Pig didn't stop the second divorce, nephew's overdose . . . & now you wonder which pig I mean. Either or, neither/welcome. First draft in finger & touchscreen, the second touching keys, wither the words like a wave to a rock/ minding its business & still washed away. Here's to less: pig, me, love that doesn't grow because you gave up watering. What did you expect? What kind of harvest is reaped w/dust & "Maybe tomorrow . . ." ? You & the bones. Always the bones.

Highwire

"The children are always ours, every single one of them,
all over the globe; and I am beginning to suspect that whoever
is incapable of recognizing this may be incapable of morality."
  —JAMES BALDWIN

He turns cartwheels in the crosswalk
on my block where "drivers"
are known to raise wheels
like planes.
   Friends in tow, two his size cut low
to the pavement & a third w/his fro
in the wind.
   They're so small, you think.
Doesn't someone miss them?
The gymnast looks up
@ your sweat through the cut
of your lawn & says "Hello"
in a voice that belies his body, like a song
born years before his run. You return
the greeting, make sure he hears you
over the hum of the mower.
      & they're off, the world
not big enough to contain the wonder
in their eyes for what they might find
on this corner, the next—all the streets
that they call home. How you find yourself
wanting something for children
who aren't your own.
   Be careful, you say,
(maybe out loud, maybe in your head)
& the next time you see them, they walk
on the telephone wires
over the street, dance high above
our same numbing days, cars

that rev & spin, drive
like stop signs are suggestions.
          Maybe they're safer on the wires
since it's not New Year's Eve & revelers
aren't sending automatic resolutions
to the sky. They turn, balance,
never miss a beat. Turn,
balance, laugh, dare one
to backflip say, "Ooooooooooh!"
when they do
like it was everything. & maybe
it is
& always
should be.

          May you see anxious cars
learn to crawl. May you know
endless cartwheels
& friends
who follow
& friends
who lead
so you can be back-
bone or tide. Whatever
keeps you free.

III.

black classical

(for my father, Dr. Robert L. Douglas Sr.)

Who
can be born black
and not
sing
the wonder of it
the joy
the challenge

—Mari Evans

The sound you hear @ midnight

is not the bass & snare of your favorite rap song

lulling you to REM,

or the fist to lunchroom table

pounding out a beat for freestyles,

it is the bass & snare

of your father @ your bedroom door,

each rap

of the wood

prying your eyelids back

to the moon.

> "I thought I told you to do those dishes
> before you went to bed, son.
> It's your responsibility.
> Get up."

The lesson: you are not slick

& he reminds you. His voice pulls you

from the room you spray painted w/subway cars

& a city skyline when he said no.

>   *There's art all over this house*
>   you say—*this is mine.* & he agrees, the walls

doused in aerosol until you leave for college

& you learn that love can be gracious,

that it can compromise, forgive.

When was he not teaching you?

        Remember:

You are 21 & he takes you for a drink

@ each of his favorite joints. You are Joe's Palm Room

representing & the smiling birthday boy

pressed to the bar @ Club Cedar

w/a catfish sandwich in one hand, a beer in the other,

& a story to tell forever. He takes you

to the places where his name holds up the walls,

adds yours

to the brick.

Remember:

You are 10 & the only Black player

on your baseball team (& he knows

what that means,

so he becomes the only Black coach).

Remember:

You are 8 & he leads you to the stove,

a pat of butter sizzling in the skillet,

wheat bread—which before that wasn't you, but you say OK—

& you are making grilled cheese

like it's the best thing anyone will ever eat.

Your friends come over to drag you to the playground

& you say, "Wait—sit down.

Let me cook you something."

Remember:

You are 7 & he turns saving your allowance

for a toy (some heavy, crazy diecast robot)

into a game, the feel

of stashing coins rivaling the joy

of the toy itself.

Remember:

Your age: a question mark. Dad

@ the turntable spinning some math

called jazz.   Your unseasoned ears

fleeing from equations he embraced

only to find them decades after

like he wasn't holding the door.

These lessons go deep in the marrow,

the sweet arpeggio Mari wrote & you analyzed.

Father, we are brighter

than any sun dare shine,

an electric tomorrow.

I cannot fill my weeping house w/enough Black Classical.

Trane, Dolphy, Mingus, & Miles together

can't fill these rooms

w/enough notes to praise you.

You are not missing. You are not absence

or echo, you are searing, AfriCOBRA

Kool-Aid colors HERE.

I didn't have to ask how you learned to give so much,

that was all Inez & Ura, the houseful of brothers & sisters

who loved hard & loud like you. Like you love our dear mother,

like I love my son & daughter, the sugar

in the living. There is no shame

in being a man of heart, in shedding tears

from fear of losing all that has led you this far.

But the lessons didn't leave w/you.

I grow to keep a kitchen clean,

a pot burning, the fish hot

& the beer cold. I stack vinyl

& keep Sun Ra rotating

like morse code to the gods.

Raised to be curious, I have questions,

like why folks always trying

to take Egypt out of Africa?

& what you gonna do

w/this art? Who is it for?

Who you gonna help?

Who?

A father's love is no abstract thing. It has a face

w/wise eyes. It stands behind you,

holds you upright.

It wakes you in the middle of the night

w/all its infinite lessons,

steadies its voice, says

    "Get up, son. Get up."

IV.

"I was born swinging and clapped my hands
in church as a little boy, but I've grown up and
like to do things other than just swing."

—CHARLES MINGUS, liner notes, *Blues & Roots*

"The work I am trying to do is a sort of
sharing with my sisters and brothers of the
world, my all; the results I leave to God."

—ALICE COLTRANE, as interviewed by Pauline Rivelli for
Jazz & Pop Magazine, liner notes, *A Monastic Trio*

Teen Age Riot

There's no reasoning w/them: your parents will not let 14-year-old you go to a Battalion of Saints show. By yourself.   In a bar.   It doesn't matter who's @ the door, who, after you buy the ticket @ Singing Dog, says, It's cool. They'll sneak you in the back. Why don't parents get it? You aren't going to drink—didn't they trust you? For parents, the worst that could happen is the first thought of what will. For any situation. No matter how reasonable. Visions of you in flames running from the bar down High Street (why you are on fire, still a mystery), Columbus cops @ your heels. Or, C.T. Skins catching a Black boy by himself, making an example of his sense of adventure. Your ticket is a sticker, black & white, w/the band logo: some kind of skull & tortured cross. You peel the back, slap it on a notebook. Save this one for songs, you think. It's the closest you'll ever get.

It Is Tuesday, & My Student Leaves Class

On a small scrap

rectangle, she says,

a friend died

& poetry class is no place

Please.

if you say, "Professor, my friend

is bullshit. Can I tell you

    Or

the canyon in my chest, the exit,

that's my friend

the sweet missing."

"Look, for real,

I'm in mourning, OK?"

Her blood, but not

try shaking a ghost's pang

the blank until your curious eye bends

folding in on itself, a hunger

It is Tuesday, & my student leaves class

        over heroin.

        of paper torn to jagged

          "Sorry,

        of an overdose—heroin—

        for an outburst."

        Stay.
        I don't care

        just died, this freewrite

        about her?

        Excuse me, I'm sure you see

        & the hallway behind me—

        boring away, she

          Or

        it ain't none of your damn business;

Not her veins, another's.

her sour. Still,

& claw. Try living under

empty to origami sky. Like night

for familiar notes of light.

It is Tuesday, & my student leaves class

                              over heroin.

On a small scrap   of paper torn to jagged
rectangle, she says,   "Sorry,
a friend died   of an overdose—heroin—
& poetry class is no place   for an outburst."

Please.   Stay.
                                                  I don't care
if you say, "Professor, my friend   just died, this freewrite
is bullshit. Can I tell you   about her?"

Or   "Excuse me, I'm sure you see
the canyon in my chest, the exit,   & the hallway behind me—
that's my friend   boaring away, she
the sweet missing."   Or

"Look, for real,   it ain't none of your damn business;
I'm in mourning, OK?"   Not her veins, another's.
Her blood, but not   her sour. Still,
try shaking a ghost's pang   & claw. Try living under

the blank until your curious eye bends
folding in on itself, a hunger

empty to origami sky. Like night
for familiar notes of light.

Universal Corner

This boy flies—in ballrooms, balancing
on wooden chairs, in a pond

of strange.   Picture
the fold of night: Iowa

in your teen age, alone & drinking
L.A.   Bathed

in silver, six strings
of Zoom, the fractured

hearts of vox & bass, once
one, now two beaks, Exene & Doe,

pecking electric mesh. Step outside,
step into your future. You are dance

in the balance, the shift & crane
for a better view, thankful

for a chair raising you eye height
to Bonebreak, punk

your forever love. No makeups, no letters
& licked stamps—13

& ears on fire. How could this number
ever be unlucky?

Getting Up

Our whereabouts murky, mired in lie. Yes, Mom, I'm staying @ Kenny's. His mom said it's cool. We paint the night, Cecil & Broadway our canvas of dreams deferred. Menace from the stoop, watch hoopties roll west, dip into the corner store for Grippos & Tahitian Treat—pretend we're somebody. Told me no & still tagged my bedroom, silver subway car & skyline talking back. How did the lash not know my name? When the sun goes down, aerosol kisses the air. Clouds whisper against a wall like our voices can't. The thoughts you see, temporarily new in the streetlamp's hush. Until another thought erases it. The paint that says nothing but silence, hand on a fat cap mouth.

Kurtis Blow Loses the Choir

A sign that it is time to leave:

Kurtis Blow, Mr. "Basketball,"
Mr. "Yes, yes y'all," knows his audience,
knows the town he's in well enough
to take his B-boy stance to center stage
stop the beat & say: "I heard you
got a lot of gangs in Columbus—how many
of y'all believe in unity?"

{Crickets}

You would've sworn AJ Scratch,
hottest DJ on the wheels of steel,
swiped his Technics 1200 needle
across every last groove
in the record that sang his name.

Aaaaay Jaaaaaay
Aaaaay Jaaaayaaayaaaay.

Cut it
& scratch it?

Kurtis continues, no sign
of ache. He is New York, seen worse
than what this rambling pack
of Midwest hoodlums claim.

I try to mimic his cool,
watch the exits, my watch.
AJ drops the needle.

Aya

I.
There's a day when you find yourself wandering illuminated aisles & wonder what you're
doing there—again—& didn't you say less trips? & this time it's products for beauty
because surely the science of what we're born w/can be reduced to problems solved by an
assortment of high-priced creams in cramped jars. & here they are: strangers looking for
things to take care of their faces: one smolder, one spark, silent steps & labored breath. &
the one whose lungs are working overtime scans the shelves for miracles, sees the figure of
sunlight & morning dew, says

"I like your tattoos; I need more."

II.
When you're in love & the person you love
        is happy & their laughter fills a room
like a tune on a music box, pin
        drum to comb, & all you want
is that note plucked once, plucked
        again—the rotation: a mercy.

III.
Sometimes I watch the news,
come across a story I wish
I'd never heard, & scream
the outcome into my cupped hands,
hope my love or my children
never have the same malaise
make a home in their ears.

IV.
Our youth—oh lord—prayer & vigil.

V.
Sometimes, I dedicate songs
to the love I wish I had.

VI.
      We're just waiting for the sky to crack & tell us what it wants.

VII.
"Thank you . . . you have tattoos?"
& the summer sunset reaches for her blouse, pulls back the collar. An infinity
sign, the new friend says, her voice still a question.

A husband in the service, one she lost—
@ home not @ war—& this mark
for him. Her granddaughter
the artist placed the ink
below the surface, closer to the heart.

"I hope you find what you're looking for,"
says the woman of exalted carve.
                  "Good luck,"
says the woman w/arms full of stories.

The aisles stay electric, their carts
point elsewhere.

"Decisions, decisions," the sunrise says glowing
to the row's end.

It's never not something.

Astral Travelling

Forgive me, matriarch. I blame my punk rock attention span, the friends on bikes chirping dreams before your portal. For a moment, the mixture keeps me still: buttermilk, Gold Medal w/out measure—the wait & reward. Millennia pass; a bright star is born in the gravity of Aries. One morning in my own kitchen, I think of you & promise biscuits to the daughter you never met on earth. I move closer to the wonder you made: the press & cut of soft planets for the pan, the way you floured the counter, rolled the dough, cut hemispheres to rise. You spread the dust again, fused the scraps, rolled them flat in the spell of creation, cut again. & again, 'til nothing was left to miss our lips. This was the science, the repetition—falling in love once, twice—that kept you going back to the dough, to the soft cut of what binds us, asking it to do more, to give another bite, to make us forget there ever was a hunger.

Obituary

The last barber I had
before the pandemic
killed like stray bullets
told me not to cut too close

on my own. "Leave
something between you
& the blade," he said.
To Donald, the student,

find your way, said the book
I signed to him. I found it
on the shelf @ Half Price. Clearly,
he didn't follow

his own advice.
               Against
the blade is all bile, no
honey—no sweet talk out

of no way: mad buzz
& hunger's wings. I am
told I can be anything, raised
by Alabama's best forged north,

housed in the bowels of the city
that doesn't love us back. Arms
& hands reached for me, take the brunt
of what the steel & sharp

dished. All a part of the language,
the oath life labors.

Christening

Five miles from Lima (the proverbial middle of), doused in a wave of nowhere, a blank squat of brick is not a rest stop. Call it chapel; call the man in cross-body rosary messiah. "With God, all things are possible"— so says the motto of Ohio. It is possible his disciples parted the sea of travelers in the parking lot & led our dreadlocked saint across hot concrete. It is possible that after the flesh parade, the faithful led the holy to the sanctuary, pushing back the door to the last stall on the aisle. His locs black as a thousand solitary nights, eyes on me, the only other Black to be found. Locked in the moment, long enough for me to dread the years he'll remain a charm for chains, how many wasted days his handlers will revel in the spectacle of his neon hem. When your mouth won't move, you understand a truth beyond pity. Fumble for lexicon, but he's gone, carefully tucked in the back of four unmarked doors, bound for the unseen, the unknown—the unraveling. Last exit on the left.

I Wish I Was as Smart as the Children I Teach

The children have done workshops on soil, flowers, & pollinators, a summer
full of contemplation thanks to church camp. I say hello, welcome
them to the tent that cuts the sun. Gathered around a table, pens
& paper there to catch their epiphanies, I ask for the shift
of image to abstraction. Listen to the word. What do you see
when you hear it? Write it! Make sure you write down objects, things
you can see, touch, smell, taste—hear. I read
a trail of abstractions:

1. Happy
2. Calm
3. Strong
4. Beautiful
5. Brave
6. Smart
7. Curious
8. Silly
9. Friendly
10. Free

"How do you touch brave?" asks a girl named Promise.

Clearly, I am not a poet. My mind
can't hold a query forged
in a child's imagination, her thought
a box tied w/ribbon & bow. The best I get
is the open box waiting
to be filled, no surprise
inside.   I go on:

    Imagine
one day that you wake up
as one of the flowers you planted:
a daylily, lavender plant, or wild-
flower). Title your poem

the name of the flower, I say, where
did you grow? What do you look like
as a flower? How do people who know
you react to the new you? How
do you feel? Head down, Promise
keeps writing as more hands
sail up. I have to remember
to keep asking questions, to call on all
who want to speak their planted pages
aloud. Promise will not be interrupted;
she keeps writing, speaks
w/ the plow of her hand.

The Punch Line

8 track & vinyl
old.
Don't have enough bus fare, I'll pay
double tomorrow
old.
Kurtis Blow "Yes yes, y'all"
old.
Just walked downtown
by myself @ 8 years
old.
Grandmaster Flash & the Furious Five
passing the torch to Whodini
@ the Fresh Fest
old.
Left my Marvel lunchbox
on the front steps of my elementary school
& found it in exactly the same spot
w/the thermos & half a bag
of stale Doritos inside the next day
old.
Fuck *Double Nickels*, it starts w/*Paranoid Time*
old.
Stuffing wads of paper
in the holes of a cassette
to record half of Prince's
"Another Lonely Christmas" off WLOU
old.
Caring about the radio
old.
Caring
old.
      Stop lying, you ain't that old
old.
The poem ends in echo

like too many good times in your ears
))old((
))old((
))old((
(& a little bit softer now)
old.

Liner Notes: N.W.A. & the Posse, 1987

Somewhere where the aerosol buoys you, floating on tags: California fluorescence. Who got can control? Who got five on this 20 sack? Glass missiles of 8 ball & Bud scrape the concrete before raising heads to clouds; Dre talking w/his hands now. Beats for days, hitting switches on six-fours & crossfaders. & you wander into the middle of this dank alley sunshine, wonder what all the fuss is about. Like, so what— they hit the studio, but ain't nobody playing a string or reading a note, just hollering on a microphone "rapping." Look: have you ever wondered what tomorrow sounds like? Like, if you could dream a soundtrack & when it played you saw the days beyond your eyes, the clouds two-step in revelry? This is it. Yes—this. Yet to be told, "You are about to witness the strength of street knowledge"—that is another prophecy for another time. "This beat so hard it said, 'What set you claim?'" one boy says & all the boys laugh. Dice signs a truce w/ cinder block walls & asphalt. The break looks down his nose behind a pair of locs, exhales smoke—asks if you're in.

Radio Free Iowa

How do I say this
w/out pageantry
in a voice

as naked
as night?
            I threw my body

over fences
after I pitched
my radio, over

& over, over
& over, until
I lost the screams

but not the fear.
I don't recall
what shoes I wore.

"Our Youth, Oh Lord, Burns Longer Than the Night" (p.5)

As my fascination with Hip-Hop grew in the late '80s, going to concerts to see my favorite groups was an essential part of forging a higher bond with the music. And who was the rapper in the King's hat controlling the stage? If you know the era, you know the answer.

"Folk Art" (p.6)

Many of my childhood memories include car rides and good music. To pay tribute to a morning ritual with my mom, I used Nikky Finney's poetry prompt from *The Ringing Ear: Black Poets Lean South* (one she gave to Lucille Clifton, no less): imagine a memory so precious that, if you could, you would wear it on your neck like a charm.

"Declaration" (p. 8)

The first of two contrapuntals: a form that naturally lends itself to this commentary on the question of who values your life.

"Poem That Begins with a Tweet About Gwendolyn Brooks" (p. 12)

The shock of a "Jeopardy" question about Gwendolyn Brooks—followed by the bewilderment of the question going unanswered by contestants—led to a poem that attempts to evolve while maintaining an element of surprise.

"It's a Demo" (p. 13)

Yes, we were *those* kids who went to Hip-Hop shows to meet the groups and land a record deal with a demo tape: rough recordings of songs hammered out with beats from a rented drum machine after school. This poem relives the experience of meeting Steady B, one of our favorite Philly MCs and the only rapper we witnessed listening to our demo. Unfortunately, Steady B went on to make some decisions with dire consequences. The title of this poem comes from the title of a song by Kool G Rap and DJ Polo (R.I.P.).

"Seer" (p. 17)

A persona poem in the voice of Devonte Hart, a child whose photo hugging a Portland policeman at a protest in 2014 went viral. The photo hid a story of abuse and betrayal that was revealed in the years that followed.

"Artifacts" (p. 19)

Living near an elementary school means kids rule your neighborhood. Every now and then, they leave things behind. This poem is about one of those forgotten items and how it takes on a new purpose.

"In Utero" (p. 21)

Not an allusion to the Nirvana album (but that would be cool, right?). Imagine explaining to your son that he attended his first Hip-Hop show before he was born. Not only that, it was ODB (who makes several appearances in the book). We are an adventurous people.

"To the Man Who Flipped Me the Bird from a Bicycle Not Once but Twice in the Middle of Ditch Road While I Sat in My Car" (p. 22)

As writers, I think we are often presented with oddities that require us to write toward understanding (a blessing and a curse). Needless to say, I was shocked when this happened on a street I drive regularly in Indianapolis. The poem is a way to examine the bicyclist's anger and its aim at me.

"Persimmons" (p. 23)

As the poetry editor for *PLUCK!: the Journal of Affrilachian Arts & Culture*, I had the good fortune of accepting Phillip B. Williams' poem "A Spinning Noose Clears its Throat" before it was featured in his debut collection, *Thief in the Interior*. A concrete poem in the shape of the title's namesake, I wondered what it would be like to attempt my own concrete poem from a different POV on the same subject. Thanks, Phillip.

"Darby Crash Calls a Dead Painter a W——k & I Rethink My Adolescence" (p. 28)

When I turned 13 and fully claimed the identity of punk rock kid, the Penelope Spheeris film *The Decline of the Western Civilization* was a sacred document. It's the reason why California was the center of my punk universe early on. But in viewing the film as an adult, I noticed something I missed before: one of my punk rock heroes spitting a racial slur—about a dead man in fact—with relative and disturbing ease. The poem is an attempt to examine a time that led to so much of my spirit and independence.

"Slow Farm Tractor Flees Police, Setting Off Slow Speed Chase" (p. 34)

One of the funniest headlines I've ever read gave way to a consideration of the audacity of the human spirit even when the odds are stacked against us.

"Mala" (p. 35)

The title is a reference to a string of meditation beads gifted to me by my partner. The beads become a way for the speaker and their partner to discuss the news of the day: a headline writing itself over and over again across America.

"ATL" (p. 37)

ODB returns, and this time the outcome isn't pretty. The concert, however, was extraordinary.

"Poetry & I Are Seeing Other People" (p. 38)

For those melodramatic "Why is poetry doing me this way?" moments—a poet's frustration, not a reader's. That is an entirely different drama.

"Ekphrasis: The Cover of Bad Brains' *Quickness* as a Map to Light" (p. 40)

This ekphrastic poem recalls a favorite Bad Brains album cover and meeting the band's legendary frontman, H.R. (if you can do a backflip on stage, you deserve that title). Bad Brains was the first Black punk band I knew anything about, the one that gave me the courage to stand tall in my punk Blackness (Black punkness?) when I fronted my own rock bands.

"Mic Control" (p. 41)

As an older Hip-Hop fan, losing favorite rappers close to my age has been an unsettling experience. David Jolicoeur AKA Trugoy the Dove is no longer with us. This poem recalls an ill-fated interview with Jolicoeur and his groundbreaking trio De La Soul during my undergrad days at the University of Kentucky. Thank you, Dave.

"Highwire" (p. 43)

Not only do I live close to an elementary school, I live in a neighborhood where drivers ignore stop signs—frequently. My frustration over this act of recklessness led to imagining a different reality for the children of my neighborhood.

"black classical" (p. 45)

Jazz, to some, is a dirty word: a crude, sensational label birthed outside the culture. The more years that pass with my love for the music, the more I realize many of my favorite artists in the genre disliked the term: Nina Simone, Max Roach, Miles Davis, Lee Morgan, and Gary Bartz among them. Simone used what she considered a more accurate moniker: black classical. This poem was written for my father–a true fan and student of the music—and read at his funeral in 2023. It begins with an epigraph from the poet Mari Evans: a Black Arts Movement pioneer he researched for his doctoral thesis at the University of Iowa that became the book *Resistance, Insurgence and Identity: The Art of*

Mari Evans, Nelson Stevens and the Black Arts Movement. Coincidentally, Ms. Mari–who passed in 2017–lived in Indianapolis and this city of poets still loves her deeply.

"Teen Age Riot" (p. 57)

Teen Age Riot is named after the Sonic Youth song on the album *Daydream Nation.* Also, I can admit now that trying to convince my parents to let me see a punk show at a bar when I was a high school freshman was not the best idea.

"It Is Tuesday, & My Student Leaves Class" (p. 58)

My fascination with the complexity of the contrapuntal form is used as a vehicle for one of the most difficult conversations I've ever had with a student. This poem can be read three different ways, each with its own unique outcome.

"Universal Corner" (p. 62)

Named after the song by LA punk icons X from their second album, *Wild Gift.* X was featured prominently in *The Decline of Western Civilization.* Soon after seeing the film with friends, X made a tour stop in Iowa City. Somehow, I snuck out to the University of Iowa student center to see them. I was in middle school, and it was my first concert.

"Getting Up" (p. 63)

The title is a reference to graffiti artists or "writers" getting their work painted in a place accessible for public viewing. Graffiti is an essential element or "pillar" of Hip-Hop culture, one I have always embraced and admired.

"Kurtis Blow Loses the Choir" (p. 64)

A poem about one of the wildest things I have ever witnessed at a Hip-Hop show (another freshman year of high school experience in Columbus, OH). This night made it clear I wasn't in Iowa anymore.

"Aya" (p. 65)

In the system of Adinkra symbols that originated in Ghana, the concept aya (strength, determination) is symbolized by the leaves of a fern. Imagined as multiple conversations happening simultaneously, the poem is inspired by what I witnessed in a meeting between two strangers at an Indianapolis grocery store.

"Astral Traveling" (p. 67)

When I miss my grandparents, I often cook things that remind me of them–an offering in food that brings us closer together across the earthly and celestial planes we occupy. The title references the famous Pharoah Sanders song.

"Obituary" (p. 68)

My one pandemic poem: a look at the casualties we don't talk about.

"Christening" (p. 69)

On a drive to visit my partner, I pulled over at a rest stop and saw something I would not soon forget. It is not often when you are confronted with the reality of freedom and what happens when it is lost.

"I Wish I Was as Smart as the Children I Teach" (p. 70)

Leading a summer writing workshop at an Indianapolis church turned into a lesson for me. These are the kinds of experiences that make me grateful to be a teacher.

"The Punch Line" (p. 72)

With a title borrowed from a Minutemen song, this poem strives for the spirit I admire in my favorite punk bands: defying convention (even by punk standards) and taking pride in being outspoken.

"Liner Notes: N.W.A. & the Posse, 1987" (p. 74)

A return to the liner notes form I explored in my first book, *cooling board*, this poem was inspired by a necessary question: why don't Hip-Hop albums have liner notes? Additionally, the Aziza Barnes poem "my dad asks, 'how come black folk can't just write about flowers?'" inspired me to push my voice in new directions. Rest, Aziza. You are missed.

"Radio Free Iowa" (p. 75)

A play on the R.E.M. song title "Radio Free Europe." Iowa City was a tough place to be a punk in the '80s (as a mob of preppy kids reminded my itfriends and me one night). The Clash was the first punk band I ever loved and the Joe Strummer epigraph that starts this multi-part poem alludes to the connection between us.

ACKNOWLEDGMENTS

Some poems in *Universal Corner* have been published in the following literary journals and anthologies, sometimes in previous versions:

Exit 7: "My Student Says, 'Damn, Prof. Where Are All the Happy Poems?'" "Social," and "To the Man Who Flipped Me the Bird from a Bicycle Not Once but Twice in the Middle of Ditch Road While I Sat in My Car"

Furious Flower: Seeding the Future of African American Poetry (Northwestern University Press): "Persimmons"

Good River Review: "Folk Art" and "Our Youth, Oh Lord, Burns Longer Than the Night"

Obsidian: "Astral Traveling," "ATL," and "Liner Notes: N.W.A. & the Posse, 1987"

The Offing: "It Is Tuesday, & My Student Leaves Class"

Quarterly West: "It's a Demo," "Poem that Begins w/a Tweet About Gwendolyn Brooks," and "Seer"

Southern Indiana Review: "Obituary" and "In Utero"

"Poem that Begins w/a Tweet About Gwendolyn Brooks" was reprinted in *This Is the Honey: An Anthology of Contemporary Black Poets* edited by Kwame Alexander.

With gratitude to Mitchell and Nia (my babies, the artists who continue to inspire me), Teneice (Love, travel, and museums forever), Mom, Dara, Camara, the Green family, the Douglas family, Breewayy, Naptown, Iowa City, my Indianapolis artist community, Indiana Humanities, the National Endowment for the Arts, punk rock, Hip-Hop, and you, dear reader. Buy that ticket and see that gig. All good things.

ABOUT THE AUTHOR

MITCHELL L. H. DOUGLAS is the author of *dying in the scarecrow's arms*, *\blak\\al-fə bet*, winner of the Lexi Rudnitsky Editor's Choice Award, and *Cooling Board: A Long-Playing Poem*. A native of Louisville's West End, he lives in Indianapolis.